WOMEN IN STEM

MAE JEMISON TRAILBLAZING ASTRONAUT

by Clara MacCarald

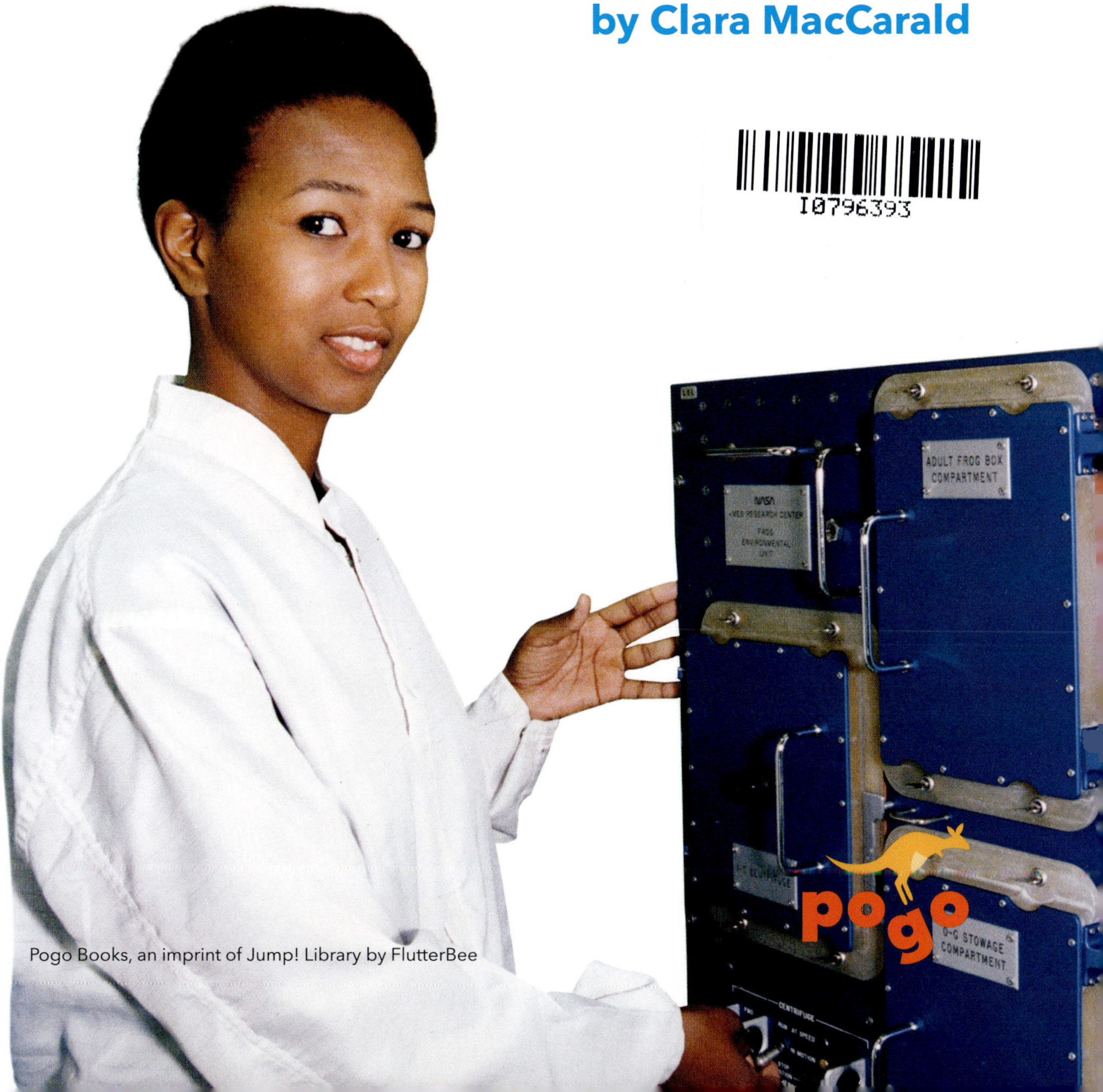

Pogo Books, an imprint of Jump! Library by FlutterBee

pogo

Ideas for Parents and Teachers

Pogo Books let children practice reading informational text while introducing them to nonfiction features such as headings, labels, sidebars, maps, and diagrams, as well as a table of contents, glossary, and index.

Carefully leveled text with a strong photo match offers early fluent readers the support they need to succeed.

Before Reading

- "Walk" through the book and point out the various nonfiction features. Ask the student what purpose each feature serves.
- Look at the glossary together. Read and discuss the words.

During Reading

- Have the child read the book independently.
- Invite them to list questions that arise from reading.

After Reading

- Discuss the child's questions. Talk about how they might find answers to those questions.
- Prompt the child to think more. Ask: What more would you like to learn about astronauts living in space?

Pogo Books are published by Jump!
3500 American Blvd W, Suite 150
Bloomington, MN 55431
www.jumplibrary.com

Jump! is a division of FlutterBee Education Group.

Library of Congress Cataloging-in-Publication Data is available at www.loc.gov or upon request from the publisher.

ISBN: 979-8-89662-379-3 (hardcover)
ISBN: 979-8-89662-380-9 (paperback)
ISBN: 979-8-89662-381-6 (ebook)

Editor: Katie Chanez
Designer: Emma Almgren-Bersie

Photo Credits: NASA, cover, 1, 10, 11, 12-13, 14-15, 16-17, 18; Dima Zel/Shutterstock, 3; UPI/Alamy, 4; Skylines/Shutterstock, 5; yujie chen/iStock, 6-7; Bettmann/Getty, 8-9; Lyn Alweis/The Denver Post/Getty, 19; Paul Chinn/The San Francisco Chronicle/Getty, 20-21; NASA Photo/Alamy, 23.

Printed in the United States of America at Corporate Graphics in North Mankato, Minnesota.

TABLE OF CONTENTS

CHAPTER 1

A LOVE OF SCIENCE

Mae Jemison is a Black woman. She has done many amazing things. She helped people as a doctor. She also went to space!

Mae was born in 1956. She grew up in Chicago, Illinois. She grew up learning about the stars. Mae wanted to be a scientist. Some people thought a girl couldn't be one. But Mae did well in school. As a teen, she earned first place in a science fair.

Mae went to Stanford **University** in California at a young age. She was only 16! There weren't many Black students there. Some teachers didn't respect Mae because she was a Black girl. They didn't think she was as smart as white men. Mae worked hard anyway. She studied **engineering**. She graduated in 1977.

DID YOU KNOW?

Mae was an outstanding student. She earned great grades. She won a **scholarship** to Stanford.

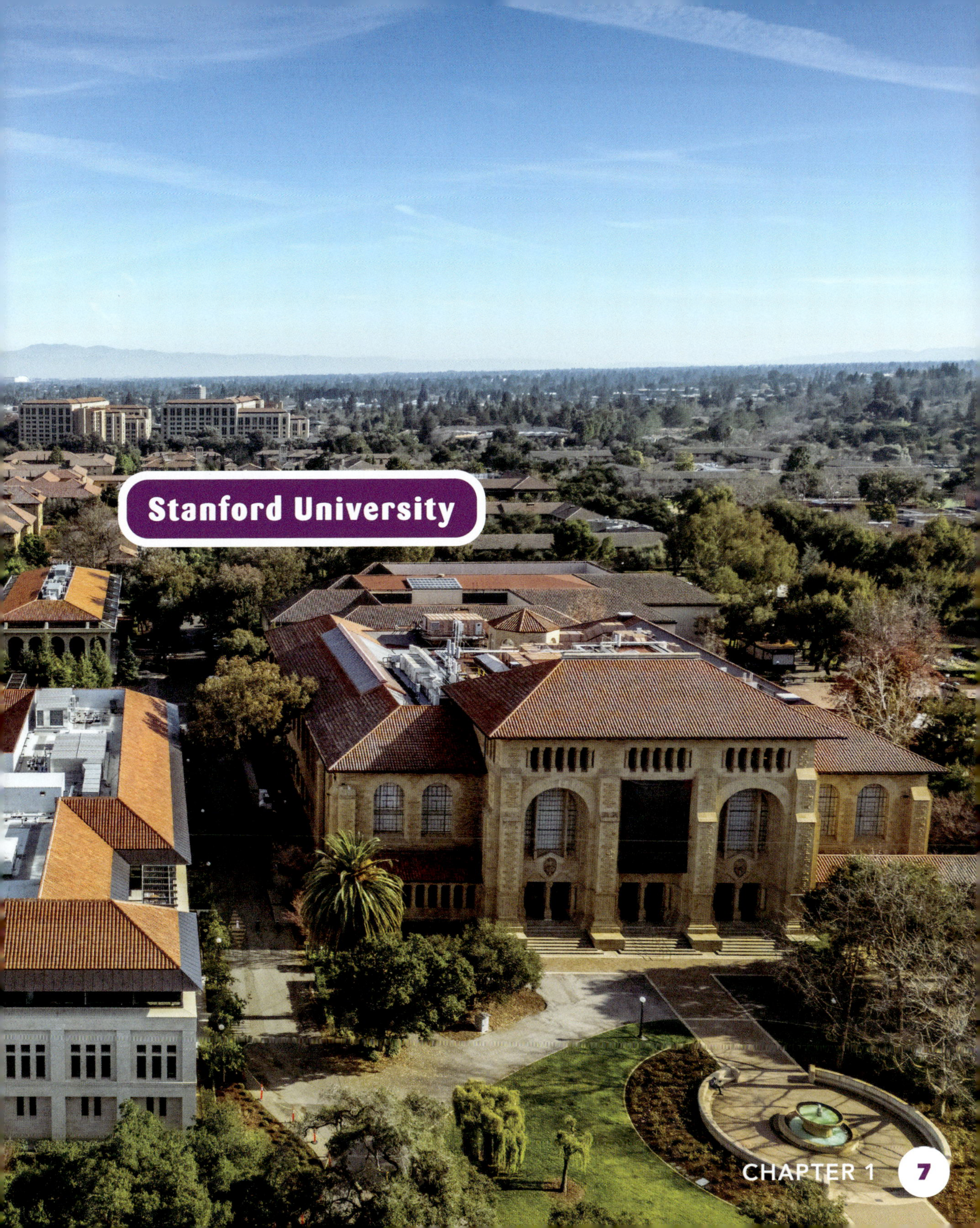
Stanford University

Mae was also interested in the human body. She went to medical school. Mae studied at Cornell University in New York. She became a doctor in 1981. In 1983, she went to West Africa. She worked there as a doctor until 1985.

CHAPTER 2

LIFTOFF!

As a child, Mae loved learning about space. Mae applied to join **NASA** in 1987. She wanted to be an **astronaut**. So did more than 2,000 other people. Only 15 got in. Mae was one of them!

Mae started NASA training. She had to learn a lot. She had to prepare for being in a spaceship.

When you jump, you land back on the ground. Why? **Gravity** pulls you to Earth. But in outer space, gravity acts differently. If you jump in space, you float! To get ready for this, Mae went in a special pool. She wore a special suit. So did other astronauts. It felt like being in a spaceship!

On September 12, 1992, NASA sent Mae on a **mission**. She and six other astronauts lifted off. They were on the **space shuttle** *Endeavour*. Mae became the first Black woman in space!

TAKE A LOOK!

What are the parts of *Endeavour*? Take a look!

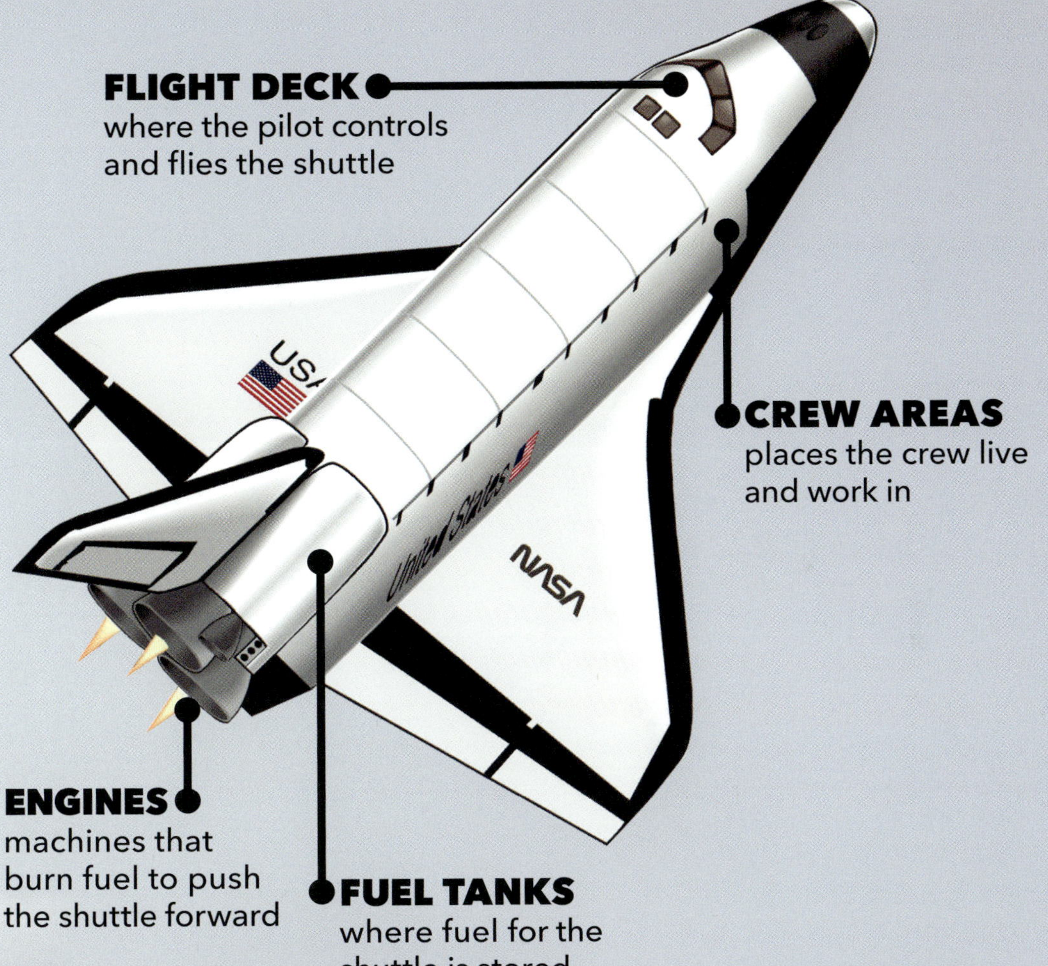

FLIGHT DECK
where the pilot controls and flies the shuttle

CREW AREAS
places the crew live and work in

ENGINES
machines that burn fuel to push the shuttle forward

FUEL TANKS
where fuel for the shuttle is stored

Endeavour had 44 experiments on board. Mae and her crewmates tested them. One experiment studied **motion sickness**. Some astronauts get sick when they feel weightless. NASA wanted to find ways to help. Mae and the others watched flashing lights. The lights made it seem like there was movement in all directions. Most felt unwell. But Mae calmed her body. She didn't feel sick!

DID YOU KNOW?

One experiment studied wasps. On Earth, wasps use gravity to decide what direction to go. On *Endeavour*, the wasps couldn't feel gravity. They didn't move at all!

CHAPTER 3

RETURNING TO EARTH

Mae spent eight days in space. She **orbited** Earth 126 times! On September 20, 1992, *Endeavour* landed back on Earth.

In 1993, Mae left NASA. She started a science camp in 1994. It helped teens around the world explore science and technology. Mae thinks all kids should have a chance to work in science.

In 2012, Mae started another program. It builds technology for space travel.

Mae continues to **encourage** people to get into science. She wants to make life better on Earth and in space!

DID YOU KNOW?

As a kid, Mae liked *Star Trek*. It was a TV show set in space. Mae got to be an actor on *Star Trek: The Next Generation* in 1993!

ACTIVITIES & TOOLS

TRY THIS!

GRAVITY TEST

How does gravity work? Find out with this fun activity!

What You Need:

- two empty plastic bottles with caps
- water

1. **Fill one bottle with water. Leave the other bottle empty. Put caps on both bottles.**
2. **Find a safe place to drop the bottles. Hold each bottle at the same height.**
3. **Drop both bottles at the same time.**
4. **Does one bottle hit the ground first? No. Why? Gravity makes the bottles fall at the same speed. It doesn't matter what the bottles weigh.**
5. **Do you think this activity would be different on a spaceship? How so?**

GLOSSARY

astronaut: A person trained to travel and work in space.

encourage: To give someone confidence, usually by offering praise and support.

engineering: The study of science and math to solve problems and create new things.

graduated: Successfully finished school or a grade level.

gravity: The force that pulls things toward the center of a space object and keeps them from floating away.

mission: An important job.

motion sickness: An upset stomach created by motion.

NASA: The National Aeronautics and Space Administration; the United States' space agency.

orbited: Traveled in a circular path around something.

scholarship: Money given to someone to pay for school.

space shuttle: A spacecraft designed to make repeated journeys into space, carrying astronauts and equipment between Earth and space.

university: A place that teaches higher learning beyond high school.

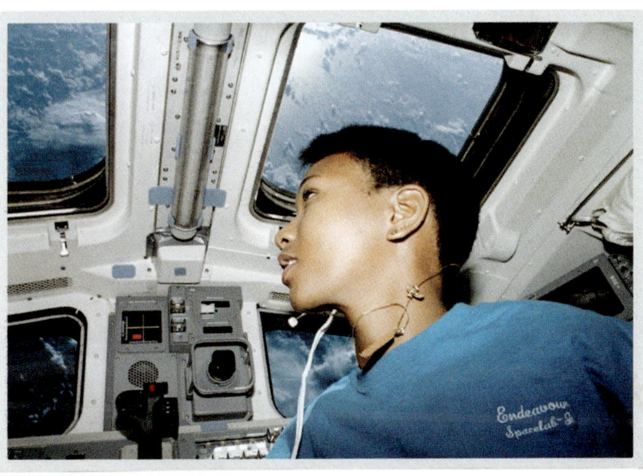

INDEX

TO LEARN MORE

Finding more information is as easy as 1, 2, 3.

1. Go to www.factsurfer.com
2. Enter "Mae Jemison" into the search box.
3. Choose your book to see a list of websites.